50
YEARS

NEW YORK SHIPBUILDING CORPORATION
CORPORATION
CAMDEN, N. J.

50
YEARS
NEW YORK SHIPBUILDING
CORPORATION
CAMDEN, N. J.

TABLE OF CONTENTS

F O R E W O R D

SHIPBUILDING, the keystone of both domestic and foreign maritime enterprise in the United States, is one of America's oldest industries. Its history is closely linked with the expansion of the nation. During the early years of America's development and until after the Civil War, the shipbuilding industry served a dual purpose, constructing vessels for both foreign and coastal trade. Coastwise shipping was a thriving part of the nation's economy, and for many years was the fastest and safest means of communication between cities and states bordering on both Oceans. Throughout this period, deep-sea shipping was of equal importance and American built clipper ships set the standard for ocean transportation.

During the transition period from the wooden sailing ship to the reign of the steel steamer, ocean trade under American flag operation fell from carrying ninety percent of our export trade at the peak of the clipper ship days to an all-time low of ten percent just preceding World War I. The shipbuilding industry, however, survived and expanded during the latter part of the nineteenth century due to a steadily growing coastwise fleet. This coastal shipping constituted the bulk of the American Merchant Marine which, at the outbreak of World War I, was sadly deficient in ocean-going tonnage.

The nation's shipbuilding industry was then called upon to build the "bridge of ships" necessary to transport troops and supplies to foreign battlefields, and the naval vessels required for these operations. Its success in these endeavors is a tribute to the resourcefulness of the industry which was forced to expand to unexpected proportions to meet the emergency of war. At the end of the conflict, however, and in spite of America's emergence as a world power of the first rank, the value of an ocean-going fleet was all but forgotten. The war had left us with a large number of cargo ships, but these were not used to good advantage and many were allowed to deteriorate and become obsolete in idleness.

The Disarmament Conference in 1922 drastically curtailed naval construction for almost a decade. While a number of notable additions and replacements were made in the coastwise fleet in the early part of this period, domestic shipping began to decline, depriving the shipbuilding industry of its previous major support. However, the passage of the Jones-White Act of 1928 encouraged the construction of new passenger-cargo liners as the foundation of a modern American Merchant Marine, while the Navy, with war clouds gathering over Europe, launched a rearmament program. As a result of these measures, when World War II engulfed the world, the shipbuilding industry was in a better position to meet demands far surpassing those of the first war. Ship-builders met those demands by creating the greatest fleet of merchant and naval ships of all time.

The New York Shipbuilding Corporation, founded in 1899, has played an important part in this contribution of American Shipbuilding to the defense of the nation in these two wars. In the peacetime years over the past half century, New York Ship, as one of the three largest shipyards in the United States, has contributed substantially to the commercial needs of the country's cargo, passenger and tanker lines, and has built a large number of the naval ships of many different classifications.

Fifty years is not a long period in the annals of men or events. Men are alive and active today who witnessed or played a part in the formation and building of the great plant now known as the New York Shipbuilding Corporation. Nevertheless, it is an honorable distinction and an achievement to have survived the economic and political cycles of the past half century, particularly in an industry notable for its violent fluctuations. It is an anniversary worthy of a review of the fifty eventful years.

The pages which follow can do little more than record the highlights of the Yard's history and the ships it has built, but hope to show that its unsurpassed facilities and organization stand ready to supply the needs of the American Merchant Marine and the United States Navy in the interest of American commerce and national defense.

THE BEGINNING

T HE New York Shipbuilding Corporation was organized in 1899. The original plan was to build the new plant on Staten Island, and the company which was formed was therefore called the New York Shipbuilding Company. Inability to acquire the desired site, however, necessitated a survey of other locations down the coast as far as Virginia. The result of investigations by several inspection parties was the purchase of a tract of approximately 160 acres on the east side of the Delaware River in the southern part of the city of Camden, New Jersey, across the river from Philadelphia. The ground conditions were especially suited to the building of shipway foundations, and railway facilities were adequate. Time has shown the selection to have been a good one.

At the outset it was decided to break away from the old century's accepted traditions of shipbuilding and build a yard in which could be applied the most up-to-date labor-saving machinery and advanced methods of structural steel construction. The planning and opening of the New York Shipbuilding Company yard was due mainly to the foresight and energy of the late Henry G. Morse, its first president.

Mr. Morse, who had resigned from the presidency of the Harlan and Hollingsworth Company, of Wilmington, Del., to form the new shipyard, was the guiding force throughout "New York Ship's" organization. He survived the completion of the yard and the delivery of the first nine ships. Up to the time of his death he had secured for his company twenty contracts. Among these was the armored cruiser WASHINGTON, first Naval vessel ordered from New York Ship.

Ground was broken for New York Ship on July 3, 1899. Contracts for preliminary work and equipment for the yard were let within a month. On June 15, 1900, in the sixth month of the new century and the twelfth month of the new yard, the contract for New York Ship's first vessel was signed. On November 29, 1900, the keel was laid.

Henry G. Morse (1850-1903)

1899 *Artist's drawing, from an old photo graph, of the 160 acre farm on the Delawar River selected as the site of the New Yo Shipbuilding Company. The old farmhouse, ne*

1900 *The new yard under construction, a picture taken on August 17, 1900. The covered ways are just beginning to take shape.*

...e center of this picture, was moved to the
...reet and is now an integral, but distinctive,
...rt of the Employment Office and Hospital
...uildings.

1901 *The yard in 1901, showing the completed ways and original buildings, with the
farmhouse in its new position facing Broadway.*

The mold loft of New York Ship showing templates made directly from layouts on the loft floor, an innovation pioneered by the yard.

There were five basic objectives followed in the designing and laying out of the new shipyard. Mr. Morse's advanced ideas were the basis of the planned shipbuilding procedure which he contributed to the industry throughout the world. They were largely the result of his extensive structural steel fabrication experience prior to entering the shipbuilding field.

First, the application of the mold loft template system for the fabrication of hull steel—a pioneer undertaking for shipbuilding at that time but now standard practice in the industry.

Second, provisions for prefabrication of relatively large structural assemblies and continuous routing of material from receipt through fabrication shops and on out to the shipways, a method widely publicized as a new development during World War II.

Third, an unusually complete overhead crane system for handling prefabricated structural assemblies up to 100 tons weight.

Fourth, a coordinated series of shops with five large building ways, and an outfitting basin completely roofed over and served with overhead bridge cranes.

Fifth, installation of propelling machinery and other heavy weights before launching, by providing 100-ton crane capacity over all the building ways.

*Installing a 67-ton deep tank sub-assembly on the
collier NORFOLK, in 1912. An early example
of the application of prefabrication, one of
New York Ship's five guiding principles.*

Of these five objectives, the first—the application of the template system—
was perhaps the most revolutionary. In the half century that has elapsed since its
introduction by New York Ship this system has come to be standard practice, but in
1900 it was looked upon with grave misgivings.

This system permitted the continuous fabrication of steel from mold loft
development of plans which did away with the previous practice of "lifting" templates
from work in place before the shop could function. Through accurate mold loft development of templates from plans, the shops are enabled to go ahead with their work for
any part of the ship upon receipt of material with the assurance that when a particular
part is wanted by the ship erectors, it will fit its appointed place.

It was because of New York Ship's experience with these advanced practices
that the yard was asked to supervise the designers who laid out and planned the Hog
Island yard. New York Ship produced the original templates for the vast fleet of ships
built at Hog Island in World War I and assisted in the development of templates for
other vessels assembled elsewhere.

The overhead crane system has been an important feature of New York Ship's yard. A complete turret, weighing 494,000 pounds, is shown here being moved by two overhead cranes.

A fundamental of the New York Ship plan is the integration of buildings to enable materials to flow from shop to ways in the order required by the building schedule.

A waterfront view showing New York Ship's distinctive covered ways under which work can be carried on relatively independent of the weather.

NEW YORK SHIPBUILDING COMPANY

Contract number one, which became the oil tanker
J. M. GUFFEY, was begun on November 29,
1900. It will be noted that the overhead crane
structure was not yet complete. Launched only six
months later, the 310-foot ship was delivered on
June 2, 1902. She saw twenty-five years of
service under the American flag, and then another
decade as the Italian MELORIA.

THE FIRST SHIPS

THE first twenty contracts built by New York Ship were secured during the lifetime of its founder. Concluded over only a three year span, these contracts included ships of six major types: the tanker, the cargo vessel, the passenger ship, the warship, the river boat and harbor craft. In the first half century of its existence, New York Ship has continued to build ships of each of these major categories. The first ship built by the new yard was the oil tanker J. M. GUFFEY. Two other tankers were among the first twenty contracts. Through the fifty years to come, tankers continued an outstanding product of this Yard.

There followed three cargo ships built for the famed intercoastal service operated by the American Hawaiian Steamship Co. All three of these large freighters saw service in World War II, although nearly twice the age of the average cargo ship at the time of Pearl Harbor.

Contracts 5, 6, 7 and 8 were for four large combination passenger and cargo liners. Outstanding in this quartet were the MONGOLIA and MANCHURIA, 16,000-ton liners built for trans-Pacific service. Among the largest ships ever built for the American Merchant Marine, both saw service in two wars.

The MONGOLIA, first passenger liner built by New York Ship. Only eleven other passenger ships built in America have surpassed her in size.

The launching of the NEBRASKAN, Contract 4, still in service 40 years later as the Army Supply Ship ROCKINGHAM.

Few ships have ever so successfully served such a variety of routes. Although laid down for trans-Atlantic trade, they were first used as trans-Pacific liners. Pressed into service in World War I, to the MANCHURIA went the honor of firing the first shot at a German submarine. After the war the 615-foot sister ships operated on the then-new intercoastal run. Sold to other interests they next found themselves with new names on round-the-world cruise service. Again called into transport duty, both ships survived World War II. Although the MONGOLIA was scrapped in China in 1947, the forty-five year old MANCHURIA is still in profitable operation as the SANTA CRUZ, running between Europe and South America.

New York Ship's contracts 9 and 10 were oil tankers, the LIGONIER and LARIMER. These were followed by barges and the fireboat ABRAM S. HEWITT, built for the City of New York and still protecting water craft and piers in the world's greatest seaport.

New York Ship's fourteenth contract was the cruiser WASHINGTON. Competition for the ship was keen. In awarding this contract to a new yard the Navy knowingly risked criticism. Despite many expressions of doubt regarding the ability of New York Ship to perform the work promptly and properly the cruiser was delivered on July 30, 1906, ten days ahead of contract time. The WASHINGTON made 22.27 knots on her speed trials, and was the fastest ship in the Navy, of that period. Not since February 10, 1903, when this historic contract was signed, has New York Ship been without Navy work.

The remaining ships of the Morse era were two dredges, another New York City fireboat, two car floats, and the ONTARIO, an east coast passenger liner. In this short period, New York Ship had been awarded contracts by the Army, the Navy and the City of New York in addition to those by private rail, oil and ship operators.

The armored cruiser WASHINGTON, first of a long line of famous vessels built by New York Ship for the United States Navy.

A bow view of the WASHINGTON on the ways March 13, 1905. She was one of the first ships of the "new Navy".

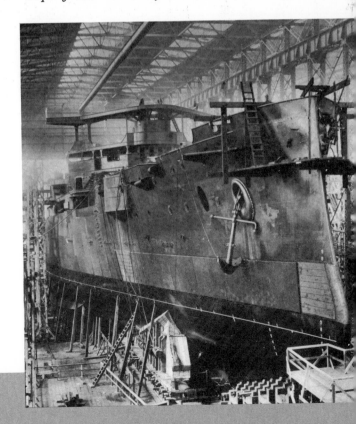

*The ROBERT FULTON, built at New York Ship in 1909,
has seen forty years of successful service on the Hudson River.*

THE EARLY YEARS

BETWEEN 1903 and America's entrance into World War I, some 200 more contracts were secured by New York Ship. As with the first twenty, these orders included ships of all major categories. In a day when few passenger liners were being built in America the yard contributed five more coastal and three river passenger ships. These were the PRESIDENT, GOVERNOR and CONGRESS, built for Pacific Coast operation; the SUWANEE and SOMERSET, built for East Coast service, and the COLUMBIA, BERKSHIRE and ROBERT FULTON, river liners.

These early years also saw increasing reliance by the Navy on New York Ship. No less than seven battleships were ordered, the KANSAS, NEW HAMPSHIRE, MICHIGAN, UTAH, ARKANSAS, OKLAHOMA, and IDAHO. Another, the MORENO, was built for the Argentine Government. Contract 62 for the yard's first destroyer, the PRESTON, was significant. As a result of the outstanding performance of this vessel many more were to follow. Less dramatic, but equally serviceable, were the lightships, car floats, dredges, oil barges, ferry boats, lighthouse tenders, revenue cutters, mine layers, colliers, tugs, tankers and freighters which were built by New York Ship during these years.

The first step of plant expansion was the building of two additional double shipways, completed in 1912 and 1915. They were, at the time, the largest ways in any American shipyard.

Long a favorite with passengers up and down the West Coast, the GOVERNOR was contract 41, built in 1907. Note the tall smokestacks, typical of the period.

The MICHIGAN, delivered in August, 1909, third of seven pre-World War I battleships, was the first of the "dreadnought" type in the U. S. Navy.

The SAMUEL W. PRESTON, first destroyer built by the Yard. She was one of the first American ships to be powered by the then revolutionary Parson Turbines and made 28 knots with 9,969 horsepower.

The OKLAHOMA, later to be bombed and capsized during the Japanese attack on Pearl Harbor. She was righted, although placed in decommissioned status in 1944. Contract 130, she displaced 27,000 tons.

The early years were busy ones at New York Ship. Shown here are two battleships, a coastwise liner and a destroyer. They are the UTAH and ARKANSAS, the SUWANEE and the AMMEN.

The ferryboat SANTA CLARA, built for service on San Francisco Bay. She was knocked down and shipped to the West Coast for re-assembly there and saw over thirty years of active service.

The SUWANEE, contract 108, at the fitting out berth. This 331-foot long passenger vessel was built for Merchants & Miners Transportation Company, and served between Boston and Norfolk.

The tanker GULFSTREAM, built in 1914, survived both wars with two decades of service in between. She is one of six sister ships built for the Gulf Oil Company before the first World War.

The collier HAMPDEN, one of twenty-one such coal-carrying vessels built by New York Ship in the early years, was delivered January 7, 1914. Like the majority of her type, she is still in service.

Transports of World War I type, later to become the backbone of the American passenger fleet during the inter-war period.

THE FIRST WORLD WAR

ALTHOUGH work continued at a war-accelerated pace on prewar contracts for cargo ships, colliers and passenger ships, most of which saw auxiliary service, destroyers and transports highlighted New York Ship's World War I building program. Substantial additions were made to the Yard for their construction. Thirty destroyers were ordered between July 11 and December 29, 1917. Eight of the first ten were laid down on the covered ways of the North Yard while new ways were being built, for the Navy, in the southern part of the original tract north of Newton Creek, and called the Destroyer Yard. New York Ship had started the construction of additional ways and shops between this site and the North Yard just prior to the war, which became the Middle Yard.

The Yard's record as a builder of passenger ships led the Emergency Fleet Corporation to turn to New York Ship for the crowning feature of their bridge of ships, a fleet of sixteen large transports, all over 500 feet in length, known as the "State" class. After the Armistice these vessels were redesigned and completed as first-class passenger liners. Delivered between August 30, 1920 and December 31, 1921, this fleet gave the American Merchant Marine 200,000 tons of modern, ocean-going ships. These required the third major addition, built in cooperation with the Emergency Fleet Corporation, consisting of four large shipways on the south side of Newton Creek. New shops, a power plant and administration buildings were erected to form another self-contained yard.

Ten of New York Ship's four-stackers including the McFAR-LAND, WILLIAMSON, BAIN-BRIDGE, HOPKINS and LAWRENCE. Completed after the Armistice, all saw war service in World War II. The McFAR-LAND in particular distinguished herself by winning a Presidential Citation for performance in the Pacific.

The JACOB JONES, sixth of the Yard's famous flush deckers, shown in the covered wet slip. Twenty-four years and one week after her keel was laid she was torpedoed and sunk off Cape May, New Jersey, by a German sub-marine.

The transport AMERICAN LE-GION being completed as a passenger liner for the South American run. This ship did not enter the military transport service for which she was originally laid down until twenty years later. This unusual view shows the "goalpost" cargo derricks, an innovation peculiar to these ships.

Examples of the two outstanding ship types of the World War I Yard program. The first of the two destroyers is the BROOKS. The transports are the AMERICAN LEGION and the WENATCHEE (later the PRESIDENT JEF-FERSON). These transports and their fourteen sisters represented the largest liner program ever undertaken by any Yard.

The IDAHO, commissioned in 1919, was long a holder of gunnery and engineering records in the Navy. Her fourteen-inch guns provided support for the landings at Saipan, Iwo Jima and Okinawa.

Three transport-liners being outfitted in the basin between piers 1 and 2, May 16, 1921. The grand total of all American passenger ships built during the inter-war period surpassed the tonnage of this fleet by very little.

The *WOLVERINE STATE*, renamed *PRESIDENT HARRISON*, passing through the Panama Canal. This liner was captured by the Japanese, although her captain had attempted to destroy her by running aground at full speed. She survived, was repaired by the Japanese and eventually was sunk by an American submarine.

The *HOOSIER STATE*, renamed *PRESIDENT LINCOLN*, saw twenty years' service on the Pacific. Now owned by Spanish interests, she is named *CABO DE BUENA ESPERANZA*.

The giant aircraft carrier SARATOGA in the final stages of construction. After heroic service in World War II, she was sacrificed as a

THE NINETEEN-TWENTIES

THE 1920s were important years at New York Ship. They were difficult years as well, for shipbuilding followed its usual cycle and declined sharply in the post-war period. The Disarmament Conference in 1922 resulted in the scrapping of the battleship WASHINGTON when nearly completed, although the COLORADO was finished and the Battle Cruiser SARATOGA was converted into the first major aircraft carrier of the United States Navy. The decade began with a good volume of work, however, for following the completion of the transports, keels for nine large tankers were laid down. Two passenger-cargo liners were likewise built in the early '20s, the MUNARGO and the CARABOBO, the latter now operating as the inter-island steamer MAYON in the Philippines.

Meanwhile operation of the South Yard and Middle Yard ways was discontinued and all building operations were conducted on the five original North Yard covered ways, as these with their associated fabricating and manufacturing shops provided ample capacity for the shipbuilding business normally available. Actually, lean years followed, in which car floats, barges, ferry boats and Coast Guard patrol boats, together with the conversion of the SARATOGA, kept the Yard operating.

Finally, as the 1920s neared their end, the Navy awarded the contract for the SALT LAKE CITY, first of the long list of cruisers which were to give such splendid service in World War II. The passage of the Jones-White Act of 1928 gave promise of a rebirth of the American Merchant Marine.

The NORA, one of nine tankers delivered 1920–21.

The COLORADO, one of three battleships comprising the last class completed under the terms of the Disarmament Conference. Until the advent of World War II, she was one of the most powerful units of the Navy.

In 1921 New York Ship built the fuel ship KAMOI for Japan. She was the first Japanese vessel with electric drive, and is shown as she left the yard. In 1932 she was converted into an aircraft carrier and was one of the very few major Japanese naval craft to survive the war, although severely damaged. Ordered scrapped under the terms of surrender, the hull will be filled with concrete and sunk as a breakwater.

The MUNARGO, passenger and cruise liner built and delivered in 1921 to the Munson Line for service in the Caribbean. Converted into a transport and renamed the THISTLE, she carried thousands of American troops in World War II.

The hydraulic dredge PULLEN, built for the U. S. Engineers' Office. New York Ship's prior experience in the design and construction of dredges, car floats, barges and smaller craft, although overshadowed in the previous years by deep sea tonnage, now stood in good stead. With the suspension of naval construction and a dearth of either coastal or ocean-going orders, the yard competed successfully in the small craft field.

The transportation of loaded railroad cars across rivers and bays is an important part of our cargo moving system. Shown is one of many car floats built by New York Ship during the twenties.

The New York ferryboat CHAS. W. CULKIN, built in 1926, one of six sister ships, just before launching.

Thirteen of the thirty-three Coast Guard patrol boats completed by the yard in this period shown at outfitting piers in the winter of 1927.

The SARATOGA, shown in the Panama Canal, is the largest ship built by the yard. Measuring 888 feet long, she had a flight deck of nearly two acres. Developing 180,000 horsepower, she had a speed of 34 knots.

The launching of the cruiser SALT LAKE CITY on January 23, 1929, first major ship laid down after the Disarmament Conference. With a standard displacement of 10,000 tons, her main battery consisted of ten eight-inch guns.

No list of great liners would be complete without the MANHATTAN and her sister ship the WASHINGTON. Over the years, these 24,000-ton American vessels carried more passengers in proportion to their capacity than any of the giant foreign superliners.

THE NINETEEN-THIRTIES

THE 1930's were years of substantial and quickly-proven contribution in vitally needed tonnage to both Merchant Marine and Navy. Compared to the years just preceding, they were times of greater activity in New York Ship's proven fields, large passenger ships and major naval vessels. The first delivery of this decade was the Grace liner SANTA CLARA, later to become the SUSAN B. ANTHONY of the Navy transport fleet. Four combination passenger-cargo liners for the American Export Lines followed, graceful and highly efficient ships popularly known as the "Four Aces"—EXCALIBUR, EXOCHORDA, EXETER and EXCAMBION. These, too, were later to become essential transports, three being lost through enemy action in the North African invasion.

The CHESTER, first of six cruisers completed for the Navy during this period, was followed by the INDIANAPOLIS, TUSCALOOSA, SAVANNAH, NASHVILLE and PHOENIX. All six gave excellent account of themselves during World War II, operating from Casablanca to Tokyo. Of these only the INDIANAPOLIS was lost, but not until she had delivered the first atomic bomb parts to the Air Forces at Guam.

Building the MANHATTAN and WASHINGTON for the world's premier passenger ship service was a noteworthy accomplishment for New York Ship. With geared turbine propelling machinery of the yard's design, these twin liners carried the American flag on the North Atlantic in competition with the largest and fastest ships of the world. They brought such luxury and performance to cabin class liner service that the leading foreign lines were forced to abandon the designation first class to bring their fare categories to a level with those of the MANHATTAN and WASHINGTON for competitive purposes. Their introduction marked a new era in Atlantic travel. As the transports WAKEFIELD and MT. VERNON, these vessels, like their predecessors, rendered yeoman service.

Four destroyers of the 1850-ton PORTER class, two tankers, and five auxiliaries completed New York Ship's record of the thirties. No navy in history has possessed ships of such size and specialization as this last quintet. Two were destroyer tenders, the DIXIE and the PRAIRIE; two were seaplane tenders, the CURTISS and the ALBERMARLE; and the fifth, named VULCAN, was a repair ship. Using New York Ship plans, eleven other ships of the DIXIE, CURTISS and VULCAN classes were built by other yards.

Framed in a giant crane, two new American Export Lines' steamers, the *EXOCHORDA* (left) and *EXCALIBUR*, are shown here at the outfitting pier.

A remarkable view of the Grace Line stean *SANTA CLARA*. The turbo-electric liner u one of the first major steamships to he gravity davits for her lifeboats.

Twenty times around this sun deck on the WASHINGTON is a mile. Thousands have made this promenade since 1933. Today she is the second-largest American passenger vessel in service.

To the left—a corner of the WASHINGTON'S smoking room, an outstanding example of shipboard comfort. To the right—the lounge—social center of the big ship.

After operating with the British Fleet in the North Sea in 1942, the cruiser TUSCALOOSA was a part of the forces covering the Allied invasions of North Africa and Normandy.

The CHESTER, which within a thirty-day period participated in engagements at Guadalcanal and Casablanca. She was also an important unit in the Battle of the Coral Sea in 1942.

The destroyer PORTER is shown here following her trial trip. The six brooms at her masthead and yardarms indicate a clean sweep of existing speed records.

The SELFRIDGE at full speed. During the war she survived an explosion which cut off her bow back to No. 2 Gun Mount.

As New York Ship was known for its World War I destroyers
and transports, it was famous for its cruisers in World War II.
Above, the PHOENIX just before delivery in 1938. Below, the
SAVANNAH at top speed of 32.5 knots.

Equally important in peace and war, the oil tankers built by New York Ship during the thirties maintained the high standard of workmanship in this class of vessel established by the Yard from the time of the first contract. The SOCONY-VACUUM, shown here just prior to launching, illustrates the strides made in tanker capacity over the years. The J. M. GUFFEY, the first contract, had a capacity of 22,650 barrels. The GULFSTREAM, in 1914, 55,400 barrels. The NORA in 1921 increased this to 98,000 while the SOCONY-VACUUM is 126,750. Now under construction as the first half century closes are three super-tankers, each with a capacity of 257,000 barrels.

The MAGNOLIA, 500-foot sister ship of the SOCONY-VACUUM, at anchor off the Delaware breakwater.

The Navy repair ship VULCAN, just after leaving the ways. Large as most passenger liners, she is virtually a floating repair yard.

The 530-foot tender DIXIE, similar to the VULCAN but specially equipped and manned for servicing destroyers.

Bow view of the CURTISS, seaplane tender AV4.

THE SECOND WORLD WAR

NEW YORK SHIP'S entire facilities were devoted to the production of Naval combatant ships in World War II. From March 15, 1942, to March 15, 1943, the yard delivered new naval construction representing an aggregate value of $217,000,000. The major part of these deliveries consisted of heavy combatant ships from 12,000 to 35,000 tons displacement, which were completed from eight to thirteen months ahead of contract delivery dates. This total output of large naval combatant ships in twelve months has probably never been exceeded by a single shipyard in the history of shipbuilding. It included three Aircraft Carriers of the INDEPENDENCE class, six more of the same class being delivered before the end of 1943.

These vessels had originally been a part of New York Ship's Cruiser Program, and were well advanced in construction when the critical shortage of carriers developed in the Pacific. In the early part of 1942 New York Ship was directed to develop designs and reconstruct these Cruisers as Airplane Carriers under top priority, resulting in the completion of nine high-speed carriers for the Pacific forces between January and December 1943. This powerful contribution to our naval forces was an important factor in the turning point of the Pacific operations.

The achievements of the New York Shipbuilding Corporation's Technical and Drafting Departments in this naval program of World War II were equally outstanding. From January 1, 1940, the Yard developed complete detail designs and working plans for seven classes of major combatant ships of 12,000 or more displacement tons, together with the detail design for machinery for an eighth class. Twenty-nine of the vessels built to these plans were completed in the Yard, while fifty-six more were built in six other private and naval shipyards from duplicate plans supplied by New York Ship.

In addition to these major ships, detail design plans were prepared and 148 Landing Craft of two classes were built as an emergency measure. Duplicate plans were supplied to numerous small yards for mass production of these craft.

The Battleship SOUTH DAKOTA

*Long known to the public only as "Old Nameless"
or "Battleship X", thousands at New York Ship
recognized her as Contract 421. When the name
was officially released, this modest sign belied
the pride of her builders.*

On December 15, 1938, four months after Munich, the contract for what
was to become New York Ship's most famous ship of World War II was signed. The keel
was laid July 5, 1939, as war clouds gathered in Europe. Originally contracted for
delivery on April 15, 1943, the SOUTH DAKOTA was actually delivered on March
20, 1942, eleven months ahead of schedule.

Those were the days of the ever-widening Japanese perimeter and the loss
of the South Pacific. Then came Guadalcanal and the desperate struggle to maintain
this first foothold of the long journey back. The SOUTH DAKOTA's first test came
on October 26, 1942 when she served as escort for a carrier in the sea-air battle off the
Santa Cruz Islands. Splendidly handled and fought by a crew which had only six
months to train, she repulsed wave after wave of Jap dive bombers and torpedo planes
and accounted for no less than 32. Only three weeks later, the SOUTH DAKOTA
was one of the outnumbered task force that surprised and defeated a powerful Japanese
fleet bent on reinforcing Guadalcanal in the all-important night action off Savo Island.
Her score was one battleship, three cruisers, and either a fourth cruiser or large destroyer.
Proving the ability to take punishment as well as to deal it out, her crew brought the
big battle wagon through this engagement with vital parts intact although she had
taken the brunt of fire from remaining Japanese cruisers and a second battleship.

Some conception of the Yard's wartime activity can be gleaned from this view (above) showing a corner of one of the five parking lots and (insert) one shift of the total of 34,000 workers leaving the Yard. (Below) Work on the ways extension to accommodate construction of the ALASKA Class.

During 1940, contracts for nineteen cruisers were awarded the Yard, including six 30,000-ton battle cruisers of the ALASKA class, although three of the latter were later cancelled. Deliveries of these ships were to be expedited to the utmost and additional facilities for the highly specialized work required by this program became necessary.

The existing turret shops were provided with an additional wing equipped with the necessary specialized tools for large turret work. The old middle Yard ways, unused since World War I, were rebuilt with new tower cranes. The outfitting basin and the five covered ways were extended some 250 feet. Gates were fitted on the ways to enable ships up to 850 feet in length to be built on all. Additions to transport and other equipment necessary to meet the emergency were provided. These extensions were made under a facility contract with the Navy Department.

Twenty-three more cruisers were ordered from 1941 to 1943 of which, following V-J Day, thirteen were cancelled, two scrapped on the ways, one delivered immediately after launching. Two additional carriers were also ordered and completed, the SAIPAN and the WRIGHT.

The turret shop, showing cruiser turrets under construction, an unusual application of the basic principles of mass production. Since 1940 this shop has produced 109 turrets, ranging from twin 6-inch to triple 16-inch guns.

The CLEVELAND, first of New York Ship's World War II cruisers. She was the prototype of twenty-seven cruisers, eight of which were built by New York Ship. She is shown here at the outfitting dock.

The SANTA FE. Keel blocks for this cruiser were prepared under the SOUTH DAKOTA before launching. Within minutes after the battleship left the ways, the new cruiser's keel was laid.

The cruisers COLUMBIA and DENVER in the covered wet slip in the spring of 1942. It was unusual for two major vessels to use this slip at the same time but deliveries were thus expedited by many months.

The launching of the INDEPENDENCE, first of nine light cruisers converted into aircraft carriers.

These ships were known as the "Sun Setters", an apt description of their role in the Pacific War.

The PRINCETON, originally laid down as the cruiser TALLAHASSEE, took part in more than a dozen actions before her loss in the Battle for Leyte Gulf.

Another "Sun Setter", the BATAAN. She was in action in April, 1944, many months before her original contract date of completion as a cruiser.

The ALASKA at the outfitting dock, a view which emphasizes the 808-foot length of these heavy cruisers. With a 12-inch main battery, they combine the speed of the cruiser with very nearly the firepower of the battleship.

Launching view of one of the ALASKA class. Of six originally ordered, the ALASKA and GUAM were completed and saw war service. The HAWAII, whose keel laying was delayed to give priority to light cruisers and carriers, was 89 percent complete at the war's end.

LCTs (Landing Craft, Tank) outfitting in Newton Creek. One hundred of these 112-foot diesel propelled craft were built in a quickly erected barge plant which reached a production of ten per week. They saw service from Sicily to the Marshall Islands.

The 150-ft. LCI (Landing Craft, Infantry) was designed by New York Ship for production at many small yards. The first 48 were built here, 12 at a time, on one of the covered ways and "launched" as shown by overhead cranes. LCI-1 received a Presidential Citation.

A crane operator's view of the carrier SAIPAN,
July 4, 1945, just before launching. Somewhat
larger than the "Sun Setters", the SAIPAN
and her sister ship were completed after the war.

The 674-foot cruiser MACON was delivered in August, 1945.

The WRIGHT, sister vessel to the SAIPAN, was launched on the day before the formal Japanese surrender at Tokyo Bay.

The WORCESTER, latest type of light cruiser, is shown before delivery on June 25, 1948. A second vessel of this new class, the ROANOKE, will be completed as New York Ship rounds out its 50th year.

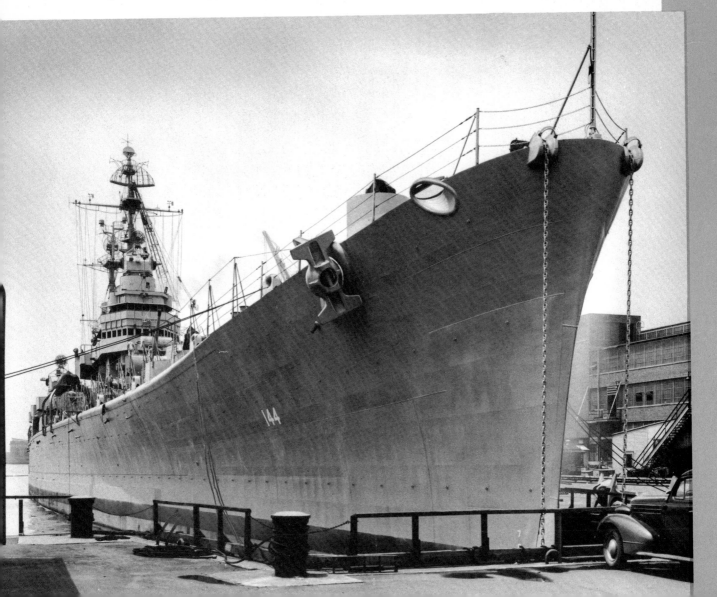

THE YARD TODAY

NEW YORK SHIP in 1949 is essentially the well-integrated plant conceived and built in the early years, kept up-to-date and completely modern in its equipment, facilities and methods. Two wars have forced its expansion to nearly double the size of the plant laid out in 1899, but these wartime enlargements serve only to demonstrate the flexibility and capacity of the organization in times of grave emergency. When all is said and done, it is the craftsman and not his tools that makes the record.

Apart from New York Ship's modern shops and machines with which to fabricate the parts that go into the ship, apart from the unexcelled shipway facilities afforded for construction, there is the skill of those who design and build the ships, the ability of those who have been trained to the most exacting standards in intricate ship construction. This is the intangible yet basic reason why the New York Shipbuilding Corporation is one of America's foremost shipyards.

The office buildings viewed from the roof of the covered ways.

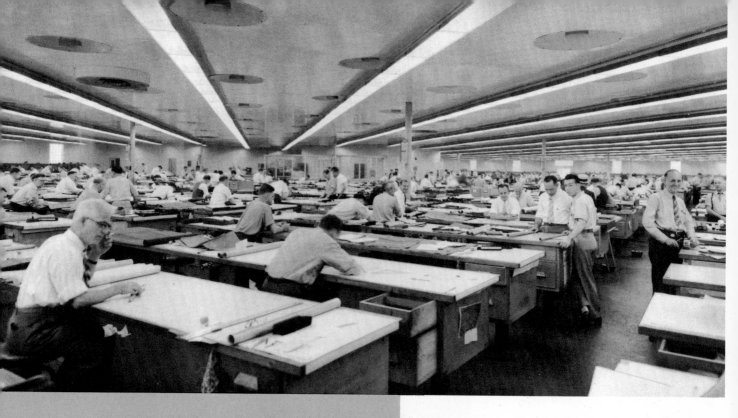

One portion of the drawing room, modern, air-conditioned, and with scientific lighting designed to reduce shadows to a minimum. At the wartime peak of employment this drawing room accommodated 650 draftsmen.

This half model of a cruiser hull will be used to facilitate the layout and ordering of shell plating. Models of engineering spaces and many detail parts of a ship are also used to determine the most advantageous arrangement.

(Above) *A small part of the Plate and Angle Shop.* (Insert) *Precision cutting a turret foundation with a machine-guided torch.* (Lower) *Bilge and bottom shell sub-assemblies for a modern car float.*

A section of the main Machine Shop, which extends entirely across the head of the covered ways. Completely equipped with both standard and specialized machine tools, work ranges from turbine blades weighing a few ounces to machinery parts weighing 100 tons.

Erection floor of the Machine Shop with the installation of blading in turbine rotors and cylinders in process. New York Ship has designed and built over 1,600,000 shaft horsepower of turbine work for ship propulsion which has set high standards for economy and reliability in service.

This 120-inch lathe with a 60-foot bed, shown turning the deck bearing of the navy-type crane kingpost, is typical of the special tools with which the shops are equipped.

A welder completing the seam of a stainless steel autoclave. New York Ship has had long experience in the application of welding and is fully equipped in every phase of this type of fabrication.

Adequate equipment to handle heavy weights is distinctive of New York Ship, not only over the ways and piers but in shops and storage areas. Here a 16-inch rifle for a battleship is being unloaded from a special flat car.

Twelve miles of railroad track and over five miles of paved roadways assures the expeditious handling of materials. An average of 512 and a peak of 893 freight cars per month were handled through World War II without demurrage due to any unloading delay.

Current work includes three passenger-cargo liners for round-the-world service of the American President Lines. 536 feet in length, these ultra-modern ships will provide luxurious air-conditioned quarters for passengers.

Three tankers, 660-ft. long, 30,000 DWT and a service speed of 17 knots, are among the largest now under construction.

Naval work continues with a high-speed cruiser of new design.

MERCHANT SHIPS

Passenger-Cargo.................	39
Tankers.......................	37
Colliers......................	22
General Cargo	7
River Steamers and Ferryboats.....	10
Light Ships and Tenders..........	18
Dredges......................	11
Car Floats and Barges............	161
Miscellaneous*..................	54

*Includes Patrol Boats, Revenue Cutters, Fireboats and Tugs.

Merchant tonnage delivered each year, in gross tons, is shown in the light colored columns on the chart.

TONS

270,000
260,000
250,000
240,000
230,000
220,000
210,000
200,000
190,000
180,000
170,000
160,000
150,000
140,000
130,000
120,000
110,000
100,000
90,000
80,000
70,000
60,000
50,000
40,000
30,000
20,000
10,000

1899 1900 1901 1902 1903 1904 1905 1906 1907 1908 1909 1910 1911 1912 1913 1914 1915 1916 1917 1918 1919 1920 1921

IFTY YEARS

NAVAL CONSTRUCTION

Battleships	11
Battle Cruisers	3
Light and Heavy Cruisers	26
Aircraft Carriers	12
Destroyers	43
Tenders and Repair Ships	6
Landing Craft LCT	100
Landing Craft LCI	48
Miscellaneous*	3

*Includes fuel ship for Japan and two sea-going tugs.

Naval tonnage delivered each year, in displacement tons, is shown in the black columns on the chart.

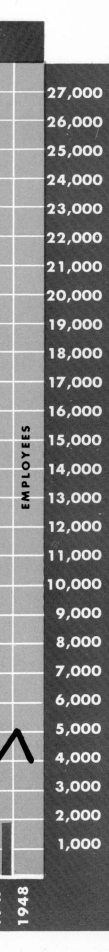

Milling and boring operations on a 95,000-pound end column for a rolling mill are accomplished in a single set-up.

WORK OTHER THAN SHIPS

MANY of the facilities of a modern shipyard are adapted to the fabrication of heavy industrial equipment and machinery not associated with the construction of ships. From its early days, New York Ship has at times undertaken work of this nature; in part in an effort to maintain more stable employment in slack times in shipbuilding, and in some cases as a public service where the facilities of the Yard provided the only readily available means for constructing unusual items. Its location on tide water, with weight-handling equipment up to 300 tons, makes it possible to load assemblies which may be beyond the size or weight limitations for shipment by rail. Precision machine tools of large capacity, ample erecting and assembling space, and an organization trained by the very nature of shipbuilding work in many engineering fields, combine to make this shipyard unique in heavy industry.

This group of modern engine lathes is typical of the well-balanced tooling in the Machine Shop.

A horizontal boring and milling machine of unusual capacity. The seven-inch spindle has a vertical travel of 10 feet, a horizontal travel of 25 feet.

One of a number of large capacity planers. This machine has a platen travel of 40 feet, and clearance between columns of 10 feet. It can readily be converted to an open-side planer for wider work.

(Left) Lowering the high pressure unit of a mercury vapor condenser-boiler into its outer shell. (Right) A condenser shell mounted on a huge positioner for welding operations.

NEW YORK SHIPBUILDING CORPORATION

DIRECTORS

OFFICERS

TECHNICAL STAFF

CONCLUSION

A STRONG American Merchant Marine and an active American shipbuilding industry are vital to a prepared America. Twice within a generation we have been forced, under the pressure of national emergency, to rebuild a merchant marine that had been allowed to deteriorate through inadequate support during times of peace. In the two World Wars of this century we have had a measure of time to overcome deficiencies that paralyzed early and effective effort. Such a rebuilding period may not be available if another emergency comes.

But in times of peace American ships must compete in world markets, and their higher initial and operating costs places them at a serious disadvantage. Due to the higher standards of living in America, it costs approximately fifty percent more to build a vessel in this country than in foreign shipyards where wages are much lower. The pay of officers and crew and the cost of their subsistence is far higher on American vessels than on foreign ships. These excess cost factors impose upon an American ship-owner a charge which he cannot carry unaided when operating in competition with a foreign owner.

The relatively small sums required to support maritime industry as a matter of national policy are widely distributed within our own economy. Eighty percent of the cost of a ship in this country goes for wages. Nearly every State in the Union contributes something in the way of materials or equipment. American ships are fueled and provisioned in the United States. The crews that operate them are, for the greater part, paid in the United States. The executive staffs are maintained in the United States. Taxes are paid here, dividends are distributed here.

Forward-looking citizens realize that it is of capital importance that the United States should carry a fair proportion of its foreign trade in its own bottoms and enjoy the economic independence which only American flag ships can give. Our foreign trade as well as our sources of vital and strategic materials from abroad, should not be left subject to the politics of competitors, however friendly they may be. Above all, the country must now realize more than ever before, after the critical years just past, the importance of such a fleet and the shipbuilding industry to complement it, as a vital part of national defense.